# *Believe it, Receive It*

## Simplifying The Teachings of Neville Goddard

By

David Allen

Copyright © 2022

Copyright © 2022 by Shanon Allen / David Allen

All rights reserved. No part of this publication may be reproduced, distributed, or transmitted in any form or by any means, including photocopying, recording, or other electronic or mechanical methods, without the prior written permission of the publisher, except in the case of brief quotations embodied in critical reviews and certain other noncommercial uses permitted by copyright law.
Printed in the United States of America.

First Paperback Edition, April 2022

ISBN: 978-1-7370946-3-0

Visit Us At NevilleGoddardBooks.com for a complete listing of all our books and 1000's of Free Books to Read online and download.

Copyright © 2022

# Foreword

Throughout this short but very informative book I intend on showing and revealing to you, the reader, that by switching words, using synonyms or understanding certain definitions just how easy it is to understand the totality of what Neville himself had learned and what he taught.

After years of reading Neville Goddard books I made a discovery that I believe not many had made. I didn't make this discovery after one or two readings. After reading hundreds of metaphysical books, I decided that Neville was the teacher for me. But I also knew there was more to his books than the average reader was seeing. It came to me after years of study and application of certain principles that what he was talking about was BELIEVING WORDS. BELIEVING THOUGHTS. I have read his 10 books so many times I have lost count. With each reading it became clearer and clearer what the underlying foundation of what he was teaching was.

I hope by the end of this book, the reader is convinced and can see for themselves, that Neville was indeed telling you that BELIEF IS THE SECRET. As long as you have an understanding of the definitions of certain words and or synonyms this should be easily grasped.

I give my interpretations with definitions and or synonyms with examples, as well as what Neville himself told us right in his books, to show that he was clearly showing us that the THOUGHTS (words) we BELIEVE are creating our reality.

This you may deny, but it doesn't make it any less true. That simply means that you are unable to see what is being said, most likely because of some previous held beliefs about what these teachings are really saying.

Have an open mind and I promise you will be able to have an all new understanding of Neville Goddard's teachings that will allow you to consciously create the life you desire.

Do you want to see Neville's teachings with new eyes? Do you want a better understanding of what he was teaching so that you can actually get results and finally know what it is to be a conscious creator?

That's the purpose of this book.

I have simplified what he was teaching and I now share this knowledge with the readers who have studied Neville but still feel as though they haven't gotten the results they thought they should have.

I ask the reader to focus, as they read this short book, on one word. **BELIEF**. While Neville used various words to describe belief, this IS what he was referring to. He was simply showing you the various ways to go about it.

Thought
Imagination / Imagine
Assumption / Assume
Persuasion
Conviction
Feeling
Faith
Acceptance
Claim
Declare

These are a few of the words Neville used to tell us how to go about believing our desires into objective existence. When you come across these words it is a good idea to keep in mind he IS talking about BELIEF. When you do that, it becomes clear what he was really saying.

As with all words it is also good to look at the context in which it is being used. There are instances where Neville may have used a word that had a different meaning than belief. That does not negate the fact that in most cases this is exactly what he meant.

Once you have an understanding of the creative power of belief you will be able to see the metaphysicians of the past who also knew THIS SECRET. Everyone who reads metaphysical books does NOT see this. You will know this when YOU learn it, apply it and get results and then see how many people actually are unaware of it themselves.

In my 14 years of being an avid student of Neville Goddard's teachings and sharing my findings and interpretations of his work, I discovered something along the way. His teachings could be SIMPLIFIED.

His message was very consistent throughout his books. We are believing our reality into existence.

**The most creative thing in us is to believe a thing into objective existence. - Neville**

This teaching lies at the core of most of what he was referring to in how Imagination Creates Reality.

To understand this we simply had to understand certain words that he chose to use.

Assumption is one word he used. Belief is a synonym of Assumption. It should be easier for the student of

Neville's works when reading the word "assumption" to know that he was talking about belief.

Assumption: a thing that is accepted as true or as certain to happen, without proof.

Belief: an acceptance that a statement is true.

Assumptions Harden Into Fact.

An Assumption doesn't need proof. The word Belief does not state this... but that is what you should know.

We are not looking at facts, logic or the outer world to determine our reality. We are choosing what to believe based on our desires, so that it becomes our reality.

I ask the reader to take this knowledge with you, as you explore the world of metaphysics, that it is our beliefs that create your reality, so that you can see these teachings as you have never seen them before and become a conscious creator.

David Allen

**"I urge you to shape your world from within and no longer from without. Describe yourself as you would like to be seen by others and believe your words. Walk in the assumption they are true and . . because no power can thwart God . . what He is imagining, you will experience." - Neville**

Assume that you are wealthy, healthy or have any other desire and believe those words. Describe yourself as being wealthy, healthy or having any desire AND BELIEVE THOSE WORDS.

Can you see how simple it is? You use words, you use words to describe yourself as you would like the world to see you and BELIEVE THOSE WORDS.

We know that Imagination in its simplest form is just THOUGHT.

Robert Collier knew this as well.

**What is imagination but a form of thought? - Robert Collier**

Throughout this book I will repeat certain things. I realize some people don't see the value in this. I do, and from what I have observed, so do many others. It's very important that we get this new understanding and not lose sight of just how SIMPLE it is.

Once you grasp the simplicity of what it means to believe a thing into objective existence you will realize there is no need for the many other methods that so many others use. That does not imply that you can't use them but it is important to KNOW that it is BELIEF that is the deciding factor in what occurs in our lives.

**All assumptions if persisted in become what the world calls reality. - Neville**

Remember, an assumption is really just a Belief.. without the need for proof.

**I do not care what the world will tell you, imagination creates its reality. - Neville**

Imagination is just Thought in its simplest form.

Imagination: the faculty or action of forming new ideas, or images or concepts of external objects not present to the senses.

Here, as an example, think of yourself as wealthy, or healthy or with the one you love, then Imagine it is already true. Do not speak of it in any other way. Do not say you are going to have these things. You ALREADY do. Be that in consciousness. Always speak from the fulfilled desire. You would simply say I AM Wealthy or I AM Healthy or I AM With The One I Love.. and BELIEVE those WORDS. Also, do not speak of these desires as anything other than already being fulfilled. The works are done once you have thought it into existence. The thought IS the thing at its conception.

**"Now I have brought you this year an entirely new series. I have named this first one — The Power of Awareness" because it is the foundation stone on which the entire structure rests. Not a thing has happened in the past year to shake that foundation. Many things have happened, many revelations, many experiments, and yet the foundation remains intact. For those not familiar with this foundation, we make the claim that consciousness is the one and only reality." - Neville**

What did Neville mean by Consciousness is the one and only reality?

Let's get a better understanding of what he means by consciousness.

**"Your beliefs, your fixed attitudes of mind, constantly modify your consciousness, as it is reflected on the mirror of your mind. Your consciousness, modified by your beliefs, objectifies itself in the conditions of your world." - Neville**

It should be very clear here that what we have to know about consciousness being the one and only reality is that it is our BELIEFS that are our one and only reality.

The foundation of creating our reality lies within ALL that we believe.. all that we accept as being true for us.

Do you see how everything is pointing to that which we state as true for us is creating our reality? That was the common theme running throughout his teachings.

Do you recall the story Neville told of when Abdullah told him You are IN Barbados? That was in the 1948 Classroom Lessons, Lesson 3 - Thinking Fourth Dimensionally.

He was referring to how to use your words, how to think. To think from the fulfilled desire, not of it or how to get there. Simply state that you ARE there.

He was telling Neville it's HOW we use our WORDS, whether you can see that at first or not.

**"For the first time in 12 years I want to go to Barbados."**

If you want to go Neville, you have gone." he replied.

That was very strange language to me. I am in New York City on 72nd Street and he tells me I have gone to Barbados. I said to him, "What do you mean, I have gone, Abdullah?"

He said, "Do you really want to go?"

I answered "yes."

He then said to me,

"As you walk through this door now you are not walking on 72nd Street, you are walking on palm lined streets, coconut lined streets; this is Barbados. Do not ask me how you are going to go. You are in Barbados. You do not say 'how' when you 'are there'. You are there. Now you walk as though you were there." - Neville

This "language" as Neville calls it, really is a language. We are not thinking OF our desire, but FROM it. Do you see the difference? It's all the difference in the world as to whether you get your desired results or you don't.

You have to have the consciousness (belief) that your desire is already fulfilled and speak FROM that fulfilled desire.

Simply... You ARE. It Is. I AM. I Have.

You do not use language that implies that there is anything you have to do to fulfill your desire.

It is done. The works are done. Your job is to think (believe) it into existence.

Don't concern yourself with "having t visualize it". If you are using the right words the right visualization will simply happen in your mind.

**"Does a firm persuasion that a thing is so, make it so?"**

**And the prophet replied, "All poets believe that it does. And in ages of imagination, this firm persuasion removed mountains: but many are not capable of a firm persuasion of anything."**
**. . . Blake**

*"Let every man be fully persuaded in his own mind."*

**Persuasion is an inner effort of intense attention. To listen attentively as though you heard is to evoke, to activate. By listening, you can hear what you want to hear and persuade those beyond the range of the outer ear.**

**Speak it inwardly in your imagination only.**

**Make your inner conversation match your fulfilled desire. What you desire to hear without, you must hear within. Embrace the without within and become one who hears only that which implies the fulfillment of his desire, and all the external happenings in the world will become a bridge leading to the objective realization of your desire.**

**Your inner speech is perpetually written all around you in happenings. Learn to relate these happenings to your inner speech and you will become self-taught. - Neville**

What did he mean by persuasion?

Persuasion: a deep conviction or belief.

Again, I repeat, the common thread in his teachings are BELIEF.

Does a firm belief that a thing is so make it so?

It surely does. And you will discover this for yourself as you put this new understanding to practice in your own life.

**"Because consciousness is the only reality I must assume that I am already that which I desire to be. If I do not believe that I am already what I want to be, then I remain as I am and die in this limitation." - Neville**

Do you recall that consciousness is modified by our beliefs? Do you recall that an assumption is just a belief that requires no proof?

Because OUR BELIEFS ARE the only reality I must BELIEVE, WITHOUT PROOF that I am already that which I desire to be. If I do not believe that I am already what I want to be, then I remain as I am and die in this limitation.

Do you see how simple it is to understand by swapping a few words?

This is what has made all the difference in my life as I applied this principle. I learned a "new language" that was foreign even to Neville when he first learned of it.

**"Once man accepts thinking from the end as a creative principle in which he can cooperate, then he is redeemed from the absurdity of ever**

**attempting to achieve his objective by merely thinking of it." - Neville**

Thinking from the end simply means the words you use are from the end. It means your desire IS fulfilled. By speaking from that place you are applying the creative principle. With practice you will realize there is nothing more to do than to create... you apply the creative principle... that is HOW we create.. there is nothing else to do that is the actual creative part of our lives.

**"You have nothing to do but convince yourself of the truth of that which you desire to see manifested. As soon as you succeed in convincing yourself of the reality of the state sought, results follow to confirm your fixed belief." Neville**

Results follow to confirm your fixed belief. That is the important part.

**"Realization of your wish is accomplished by assuming the feeling of the wish fulfilled. You cannot fail unless you fail to convince yourself of the reality of your wish. A change of belief is confirmed by a change of expression." - Neville**

It is very important that you understand what Neville meant by feeling.

The quote above SHOULD tell you that "assuming the feeling of the wish fulfilled" is SIMPLY to believe that your wish is fulfilled. You DO NOT HAVE TO FEEL ANY EMOTION when you SAY IT. That is a fallacy... BELIEVE IT FIRST... stay in that state... persist in that state... THEN you will feel the emotion of it.

**"When I speak of feeling I do not mean emotion, but the acceptance of the fact that the desire is fulfilled." - Neville**

Acceptance of the fact that the desire is fulfilled means that you BELIEVE that your desire is fulfilled.

With the right interpretation of certain words it gives you a completely different understanding. With the right interpretation you will be AMAZED as you see what is being said as opposed to only thinking you know what was said.

You are BELIEIVNG things into objective existence.

What that comes down to is you are BELIEVING WORDS.

You use words to describe your fulfilled desire and believe those words.

Here is another example where he uses Acceptance.

**"I know of no clearer definition of the means by which we realize our desires than to experience in imagination, what we would experience in the flesh, were we to achieve our goal. This imaginary experience of the end with acceptance, wills the means. The fourth-dimensional Self then constructs with its larger outlook the means necessary to realize the accepted end." - Neville**

Acceptance: the act of assenting or believing.

This imaginary experience of the end with BELIEF, wills the means.

Simply experience in THOUGHT what you would experience in the flesh, believe those words and this imaginary experience of the end, that you believe, wills the means.

**"The undisciplined mind finds it difficult to assume a state which is denied by the senses." - Neville**

The undisciplined mind finds it difficult to BELIEVE a state which is denied by the senses.

What does it mean to believe a state?

Think of your fulfilled desire as the state being spoken of. Simply believe your desire is fulfilled.

**"Prayers to be successful must be claiming rather than begging, so if you would pray for riches turn from your picture of poverty by denying the very evidence of your senses and assume the nature of being wealthy." - Neville**

Here we have an example of him using "claiming" which can more easily understood as Believing.

Prayers to be successful must be BELIEVING rather than begging, so if you would pray for riches turn from your picture of poverty by denying the very evidence of your senses and assume the nature of being wealthy (which is to simply believe that you are wealthy).

**Your consciousness, modified by your beliefs, objectifies itself in the conditions of your world." - Neville**

This was posted earlier. But I want to stress to the student how to better understand what Neville meant by "consciousness".

Since consciousness is modified by our beliefs just think of it as the sum total of ALL YOU BELIEVE. Don't worry, the subconscious keeps track of ALL our beliefs.

You will see, as you read his books, where this will benefit you greatly in getting a better understanding of his teachings.

**"The word, or desire, must be fixed or united with consciousness to give it reality." - Neville**

Your words must be fixed or united with your beliefs to give them reality.

**"Now here is something to always bear in mind.**

*"You cannot put new wine in old bottles or new patches upon old garments."*

**That is; you cannot take with you into the new consciousness any part of the old man. All of your present beliefs, fears and limitations are weights that bind you to your present level of consciousness. If you would transcend this level you must leave behind all that is now your present self, or conception of yourself." - Neville**

You can't hold on to your old beliefs while establishing new beliefs. You must renew your mind. Renew your beliefs.

Example: If it is wealth that you desire you can't hold on to any belief that wealth is not already yours WHILE at the same time affirming that you are wealthy.

Let go of all any and all beliefs that deny that you are already wealthy.

Do not speak of not having money in any form.

**"The only way to change your expressions of life is to change your consciousness. For consciousness is the reality that eternally solidifies itself in the things round about you." - Neville**

Again, we know that consciousness is modified by our beliefs. So let's read this again with that info.

The only way to change your expressions of life is to change your BELIEFS. For YOUR BELIEFS ARE the reality that eternally solidifies itself in the things round about you.

Now isn't that amazing to be able to see and understand that? It is no longer mysterious.

**"Man's world in its every detail is his consciousness out-pictured. Your environment, and all within it, reflects that which you are in consciousness. As long as you continue to be that in consciousness so long will you continue to out-picture it in your world." - Neville**

Man's world in its every detail is his BELIEFS out-pictured. Your environment, and all within it, reflects that which you BELIEVE. As long as you continue to BELIEVE WHAT YOU BELIEVE so long will you continue to out-picture it in your world.

Isn't it amazing that by simply having a better definition that we are able to have a better understanding?

**"I AM" is an open door for all that I AM to enter. Your awareness of being is lord and shepherd of your life.**

**So,**

*"The Lord is my shepherd; I shall not want"*

**is seen in its true light now to be your consciousness. You could never be in want of proof or lack the evidence of that which you are aware of being.**

**This being true, why not become aware of being great; God-loving; wealthy; healthy; and all attributes that you admire?**

**It is just as easy to possess the consciousness of these qualities as it is to possess their opposites for you have not your present consciousness because of your world. On the contrary, your world is what it is because of your present consciousness.**

**Simple, is it not? Too simple in fact for the wisdom of man that tries to complicate everything. - Neville**

I would like to make 2 references here to what Neville meant by "I AM" (at least one definition he used).

"I AM" or the awareness of being is the only reality.

Consciousness is the only reality.

Take a moment to see what this is saying so we can interpret that excerpt.

YOUR BELIEFS ARE an open door for all that I AM to enter. YOUR BELIEFS ARE lord and shepherd of your life.

So,

*"MY BELIEFS ARE my shepherd; I shall not want"*

is seen in its true light now to be your consciousness. You could never be in want of proof or lack the evidence of that which you BELIEVE.

This being true, why not become aware of being great; God-loving; wealthy; healthy; and all attributes that you admire?

It is just as easy to possess the BELIEF IN these qualities as it is to BELIEVE IN their opposites for you have not your present BELIEFS because of your world. On the contrary, your world is what it is because of your present BELIEFS.

Simple, is it not? Too simple in fact for the wisdom of man that tries to complicate everything.

Again, I find this amazing. This is exactly how I gained understanding and have been able to apply this knowledge to prove to myself that Neville was indeed giving us the truth of how we create our reality.

**"It was in the fall of 1933 in New York City that I approached Abdullah with a problem. He asked me one simple question,**

**"What do you want?" I told him that I would like to spend the winter in Barbados, but that I was broke. I literally did not have a nickel.**

**"If you will imagine yourself to be in Barbados", said he, "thinking and viewing the world from that state of consciousness instead of thinking of Barbados, you will spend the winter there."**

"You must not concern yourself with the ways and means of getting there, for the state of consciousness of already being in Barbados, if occupied by your imagination, will devise the means best suited to realize itself."

Man lives by committing himself to invisible states, by fusing his imagination with what he knows to be other than himself, and in this union he experiences the results of that fusion. No one can lose what he has, save by detachment from the state where the things experienced have their natural life.

"You must imagine yourself right into the state of your fulfilled desire", Abdullah told me, "and fall asleep viewing the world from Barbados."

The world which we describe from observation must be as we describe it relative to ourselves.

Our imagination connects us with the state desired. But we must use imagination masterfully, not as an onlooker thinking of the end, but as a partaker thinking from the end. We must actually be there in imagination.

If we do this, our subjective experience will be realized objectively." - Neville

Do you recall this story? What do you think Neville was saying when relaying one of his stories about Abdullah? He was referring to our WORDS creating our reality.

Remember this?

"As you walk through this door now you are not walking on 72nd Street, you are walking on palm lined streets, coconut lined streets; this is Barbados.

**Do not ask me how you are going to go. You are in Barbados. You do not say 'how' when you 'are there'. You are there. Now you walk as though you were there."**

You are IN Barbados. That means you do not use any words that say otherwise. I AM In Barbados. Don't concern yourself with how you get there. Remember, imagination fulfills itself.

**"I say imagination creates reality, and if this premise is true then imagination fulfills itself in what your life becomes. Although I have changed the words, what I am saying is not new. Scripture says it in this manner: "Whatsoever you desire, believe you have received it and you will." This statement goes back two thousand years, yet even before that Jeremiah tells of the same principle in his story of the potter and his clay." - Neville**

We use our imagination... which is really in its simplest form.. our thought. So with that knowledge, we KNOW that THOUGHT FULFILLS ITSELF.

As far as creation goes there really is nothing more to do than to speak (think) it into existence... and accept that your words are true... which is all belief is.

**"You have nothing to do but convince yourself of the truth of that which you desire to see manifested." - Neville**

It should be noted that anything we do should be in harmony with what we believe. If you believe that you are successful then you would act successful.

**"Each garment has certain limitations. In order to transcend these limitations and give expression to**

**that which, as man, John Smith, you find yourself incapable of doing, you take your attention away from your present limitations, or John Smith conception of yourself, and merge yourself in the feeling of being that which you desire. Just how this desire or newly attained consciousness will embody itself, no man knows. For I, or the newly attained consciousness, has ways that ye know not of; its ways are past finding out."** - Neville

Here, once again, as throughout his teachings, he is talking about belief. Limitations, conception of yourself, feeling of being that which you desire and consciousness are all about your beliefs.

Let's interpret this excerpt with that knowledge.

Each garment has certain LIMITING BELIEFS. In order to transcend these LIMITING BELIEFS and give expression to that which, as man, John Smith, you find yourself incapable of doing, you take your attention away from your present LIMITING BELIEFS, or John Smith BELIEF ABOUT yourself, and merge yourself in the BELIEF THAT YOU ARE that which you desire. Just how this desire or newly attained BELIEF will embody itself, no man knows. For I, or the newly attained BELIEF, has ways that ye know not of; its ways are past finding out.

See what a difference it makes in not only understanding but seeing how easy it is to apply the right knowledge that gives us results?

**"If you have not the consciousness of the thing, you have not the cause or foundation upon which thing is erected." A proof of this established consciousness is given you in the words, "Thank you, father." When you come into the joy of**

**thanksgiving so that you actually feel grateful for having received that which is not yet apparent to the senses, you have definitely become one in consciousness with the thing for which you gave thanks.- Neville**

Simple interpretation.

If you have not the BELIEF OF BEING the thing, you have not the cause or foundation upon which thing is erected. A proof of this established BELIEF is given you in the words, "Thank you, father." When you come into the joy of thanksgiving so that you actually feel grateful for having received that which YOU BELIEVE, BUT is not yet apparent to the senses, you have definitely become one WITH YOUR BELIEF AND the thing for which you gave thanks.

When I first made this discovery of being able to see just how many words Neville used could be switched with BELIEF I felt like a light went on and I could see clearly what he was saying. It changed my whole understanding. It gave me something I could work with and apply. Now I knew it really came down to the thoughts (words) I believed that were in fact creating my reality.

*"You are told,*
*"He who lacks wisdom let him ask of God,*
*that gives to all liberally, and upbraideth not;*
*and it shall be given unto him.*
*But let him ask not doubting*
*for he who doubts is as a wave of the sea*
*that is tossed and battered by the winds.*
*And let not such a one think that*
*he shall receive anything from the Lord."*

You can see why this statement is made, for only upon the rock of faith can anything be established. If you have not the consciousness of the thing, you have not the cause or foundation upon which thing is erected.

A proof of this established consciousness is given you in the words,

> *"Thank you, father."*

When you come into the joy of thanksgiving so that you actually feel grateful for having received that which is not yet apparent to the senses, you have definitely become one in consciousness with the thing for which you gave thanks.

> God (your awareness) is not mocked.

You are ever receiving that which you are aware of being and no man gives thanks for something which he has not received.

> *"Thank you father"*

is not, as it is used by many today a sort of magical formula.

> You need never utter aloud the words,

> *"Thank you, father."*

In applying this principle as you rise in consciousness to the point where you are really grateful and happy for having received the thing desired, you automatically rejoice and give thanks inwardly. You have already accepted the gift which was but a desire before you rose in consciousness,

**and your faith is now the substance that shall clothe your desire.**

**This rising in consciousness is the spiritual marriage where two shall agree upon being one and their likeness or image is established on earth.**

*"For whatsoever ye ask in my name the same give I unto you." - Neville*

Here again we see he is talking about believing. We know this because he told us that consciousness is modified by our beliefs. So that is exactly what we should be aware of every time we see him speaking of consciousness.

"You are told,
*"He who lacks wisdom let him ask of God,
that gives to all liberally, and upbraideth not;
and it shall be given unto him.
But let him ask not doubting
for he who doubts is as a wave of the sea
that is tossed and battered by the winds.
And let not such a one think that
he shall receive anything from the Lord."*

You can see why this statement is made, for only upon YOUR PERSISTENT CONVICTION THAT WHAT YOU SAY IS TRUE, IS TRUE can anything be established. If you have not the BELIEF of the thing, you have not the cause or foundation upon which thing is erected.

A proof of this established CONVICTION (BELIEF) is given you in the words,

*"Thank you, father."*

When you come into the joy of thanksgiving so that you actually feel grateful for having received that which is not yet apparent to the senses, you have definitely become one WITH YOUR BELIEF AND the thing for which you gave thanks.

God (your awareness) is not mocked.

You are ever receiving that which you BELIEVE YOU ARE and no man gives thanks for something which he has not received.

*"Thank you father"*

is not, as it is used by many today a sort of magical formula.

You need never utter aloud the words,

*"Thank you, father."*

In applying this principle as you ACCEPT THAT YOUR BELIEF IS NOW YOUR REALITY where you are really grateful and happy for having received the thing desired, you automatically rejoice and give thanks inwardly. You have already accepted the gift which was but a desire before you ACCEPTED IT, and your faith is now the substance that shall clothe your desire.

This ACCPETING YOUR BELIEF AS YOUR REALITY is the spiritual marriage where two shall agree upon being one and their likeness or image is established on earth.

*"For whatsoever ye ask in my name the same give I unto you."*

Note: Asking in his name means to claim your desire. To believe that which you state is true, IS true. I AM

That... the thing desired, I AM. You believe you already ARE what you desire to be.

**"I AM" the vine and ye are the branches."**

**Consciousness is the 'vine,' and those qualities which you are now conscious of being are as 'branches' that you feed and keep alive.**

**Just as a branch has no life except it be rooted in the vine, so likewise things have no life except you be conscious of them. Just as a branch withers and dies if the sap of the vine ceases to flow towards it, so do things in your world pass away if you take your attention from them, because your attention is as the sap of life that keeps alive and sustains the things of your world. - Neville**

*"I AM" the vine and ye are the branches."*

YOUR BELIEFS ARE the 'vine,' and those qualities which you NOW BELIEVE are as 'branches' that you feed and keep alive.

Just as a branch has no life except it be rooted in the vine, so likewise things have no life except you BELIEVE THEM TO BE TRUE FOR YOU. Just as a branch withers and dies if the sap of the vine ceases to flow towards it, so do things in your world pass away if you take your attention from them BY NO LONGER BELIVING THEM TO BE TRUE FOR YOU, because your attention is as the sap of life that keeps alive and sustains the things of your world.

**"For signs follow, they do not precede.**

**To constantly kick and complain against the limitations of poverty while remaining poor in**

consciousness is to play the fool's game. Changes cannot take place from that level of consciousness for life in constantly out picturing all levels.

Follow the example of the prodigal son. Realize that you, yourself brought about this condition of waste and lack and make the decision within yourself to rise to a higher level where the fatted calf, the ring, and the robe await your claim.

There was no condemnation of the prodigal when he had the courage to claim this inheritance as his own. Others will condemn us only as long as we continue in that for which we condemn ourselves.

**So:**

*"Happy is the man that condemneth himself not in that which he alloweth."*

For to life nothing is condemned. All is expressed.

Life does not care whether you call yourself rich or poor; strong or weak. It will eternally reward you with that which you claim as true of yourself." - Neville

For signs follow YOUR BELIEFS, they do not precede THEM.

To constantly kick and complain against the limitations of poverty while BELIEVING YOURSELF TO BE POOR is to play the fool's game. Changes cannot take place from that level of consciousness, WHERE YOU BELIEVE YOU ARE POOR, for life in constantly out-picturing all levels.

Follow the example of the prodigal son. Realize that you, yourself brought about this condition of waste and lack

BY BELIEVING YOURSELF TO BE POOR, BY CLAIMING YOURSELF TO BE POOR and make the decision within yourself to rise to a higher level where the fatted calf, the ring, and the robe await your claim BY STATING THAT YOU ARE WEALTHY.

There was no condemnation of the prodigal when he had the courage to claim this inheritance as his own (YOUR INHERITANCE IS YOUR BELIEFS). Others will SEE US AS POOR only as long as we continue TO CLAIM THAT WE ARE POOR.

So:

*"Happy is the man that condemneth himself not in that which he alloweth."*

For to life nothing is condemned. All is expressed.

Life does not care whether you call yourself rich or poor; strong or weak. It will eternally reward you with that which you claim as true of yourself.

**"Have faith in this unseen claim until the conviction is born within you that it is so. Your confidence in this claim will pay great rewards.**

**Just a little while and he, the thing desired, will come. But without faith it is impossible to realize anything. Through faith the worlds were framed because**

*"faith is the substance of the thing hoped for, the evidence of the thing not yet seen."*

**Don't be anxious or concerned as to results. They will follow just as surely as day follows night.**

**Look upon your desires, all of them, as the spoken words of God, and every word or desire a promise.**

**The reason most of us fail to realize our desires is because we are constantly conditioning them. Do not condition your desire. Just accept it as it comes to you. Give thanks for it to the point that you are grateful for having already received it, then go about your way in peace.**

**Such acceptance of your desire is like dropping seed, fertile seed, into prepared soil.**

**For when you can drop the thing desired in consciousness, confident that it shall appear, you have done all that is expected to you." - Neville**

Have faith in YOUR unseen BELIEF until the conviction is born within you that it is so. Your confidence in YOUR BELIEFS will pay great rewards.

Just a little while and he, THAT WHICH YOU DESIRE TO BE TRUE FOR YOU, will come. But without PERSISTENT BELIEF (Faith) it is impossible to realize anything. Through PERSISTENT BELIEF the worlds were framed because

> *"faith is the substance of the thing hoped for, the evidence of the thing not yet seen."*

Don't be anxious or concerned as to results. They will follow just as surely as day follows night.

Look upon your BELIEFS, all of them, as the spoken words of God, and every word or desire a promise.

The reason most of us fail to realize our desires is because we are constantly conditioning them. Do not condition your desire. Just BELIEVE IT TO BE TRUE FOR YOU NOW. Give thanks for it to the point that you are grateful for having already received it, then go about your way in peace.

Such acceptance of your desire is like dropping seed, fertile seed, into prepared soil.

For when you BELIEVE YOUR DESIRE TO ALREADY BE TRUE, confident that it shall appear, you have done all that is expected to you.

**"Deny it if you will, it still remains a fact that consciousness is the only reality and things but mirror that which you are in consciousness. So the heavenly state you are seeking will be found only in consciousness, for the kingdom of heaven is within you." - Neville**

Deny it if you will, it still remains a fact that YOUR BELIEFS ARE the only reality FOR YOU and things but mirror that which you BELIEVE TO BE TRUE FOR YOU. So the heavenly state you are seeking will be found only in YOUR CHOSEN BELIEFS, for the kingdom of heaven is within you

**"Successful realization of the thing desired is also told us in the story of Daniel in the lion's den.**

**Here, it is recorded that Daniel, while in the lion's den, turned his back upon the lions and looked towards the light coming from above; that the lions remained powerless and Daniel's faith in his God saved him.**

**This also is your story and you too must do as Daniel did.**

**If you found yourself in a lion's den you would have no other concern but lions. You would not be thinking of one thing in the world but your problem, which problem would be lions.**

**Yet, you are told that Daniel turned his back upon them and looked towards the light that was his God.**

**If we would follow the example of Daniel we would, while imprisoned within the den of poverty of sickness, take our attention away from our problems of debts or sickness and dwell upon the thing we seek.**

**If we do not look back in consciousness to our problems but continue in faith, believing ourselves to be that which we seek, we too will find our prison walls open and the thing sought, yes, "whatsoever things", realized." - Neville**

Do you see here that he is CLEARLY talking about our beliefs... that which w state as being true for us?

This is a story, an analogy. The lions represent your limiting beliefs. Simply stop believing that you are limited... which means thinking thoughts.. using words that state that you are limited. This is easily done with practice. THAT is how easy it is to "turn your back" on your limiting beliefs.

Live in the state of already having your desires and stop using words (silent or spoken) that imply that they aren't already fulfilled. You will be amazed by living this way just how much life changes for you.

**"Verily, verily, I say unto you, before Abraham was, I AM."**

> *"In the beginning was the Word, and the Word was with God, and the Word was God"*

**In the beginning was the unconditioned awareness of being, and the unconditioned awareness of being became conditioned by imagining itself to be something, and the unconditioned awareness of being became that which it had imagined itself to be; so did creation begin." - Neville**

**By this law, first conceiving, then becoming that conceived, all things evolve out of nothing; and without this sequence there is not anything made that is made.**

> *"Verily, verily, I say unto you, before Abraham was, I AM."*

> *"In the beginning was the Word, and the Word was with God, and the Word was God"*

In the beginning was the unconditioned awareness of being, and the unconditioned awareness of being became conditioned by BELIEVING itself to be something, and the unconditioned awareness of being became that which it had BELIEVED itself to be; so did creation begin.

By this law, first THINKING OF YOUR DESIRE, then becoming that THAT WHICH YOU THOUGHT, BY BELIEVING YOU ARE THAT, all things evolve out of nothing; and without this sequence there is not anything made that is made.

Think you are successful, believe you are successful and your success will evolve out of your BELIEF.

At this point in this book can you see the underlying thread in the majority of what Neville was writing about?

All true metaphysicians knew the power of BELIEF. To say otherwise doesn't make it any less true, it just means that YOU can't be a conscious creator by consciously choosing that which you believe to be true and are still living out of your sense perceptions, and accepting that as your reality.

It is no coincidence that ONE WORD.. BELIEF.. can be seen and inserted into so many metaphysical books as a synonym of what these teachers were teaching. Many teachers just used a different writing style, but once you see this as the foundation of what the REAL SECRET is it will enlighten you to what the FEW knew throughout the centuries.

**"Man can decree a thing and it will come to pass.**

**Man has always decreed that which has appeared in his world. He is today decreeing that which is appearing in his world and he shall continue to do so as long as man is conscious of being man.**

**Nothing has ever appeared in man's world, but what man decreed that it should. This you may deny; but try as you will, you cannot disprove it for this decreeing is based upon a changeless principle." - Neville**

Here we have the word "decree". What does it mean to "decree"?

When we look up synonyms for decree we find that one of them is "instruction" So we are basically giving instructions? Who or what are we giving instructions to? Our subconscious mind. Now the important thing here is to know HOW to give these instructions. That is very important.

Our BELIEFS are instructions.

We don't give instructions to the subconscious mind like we would give to another person. The subconscious responds to our BELIEFS... those words we accept as being true for us.

So let's interpret that excerpt.

> Man can GIVE INSTRUCTIONS, BELIEVE A THING TO BE TRUE FOR HIM, and it will come to pass.

Man has always GIVEN INSTRUCTIONS that which has appeared in his world. He is today BELIEVING that which is appearing in his world and he shall continue to do so as long as man is conscious of being man.

Nothing has ever appeared in man's world, but what man HAS STATED AS BEING TRUE FOR HIM. This you may deny; but try as you will, you cannot disprove it for this BELIEVING is based upon a changeless principle.

**"When man discovers his consciousness to be the impersonal power of expression, which power eternally personifies itself in his conceptions of himself, he will assume and appropriate that state of consciousness which he desires to express; in so doing he will become that state in expression." - Neville**

When man discovers HIS BELIEFS to be the impersonal power of expression, which power eternally personifies itself in his conceptions of himself, he will assume and appropriate HIS CHOSEN BELIEFS which he desires to express; in so doing he will become that state in expression.

Remember, YOUR beliefs do not need proof. YOU are the authority as to what is true for you. When YOU say something is true for you, it has been decreed and that order will be carried out. Who or what carries out this order? Your subconscious mind.

> "**The law of consciousness is the only law of expression.**
>
> *"I AM the way".*
>
> *"I AM the resurrection".*

**Consciousness is the way as well as the power which resurrects and expresses all that man will ever be conscious of being.**

**Turn from the blindness of the uninitiated man who attempts to express and possess those qualities and things which he is not conscious of being and possessing; and be as the illumined mystic who decrees, on the basis of this changeless law.**

**Consciously claim yourself to be that which you seek; appropriate the consciousness of that which you see; and you too will know the status of the true mystic, as follows:**

I became conscious of being it. I am still conscious of being it. And I shall continue to be conscious of being it until that which I am conscious of being is perfectly expressed.

> **"Yes, I shall decree a thing and it shall come to pass." - Neville.**

I love this one. No matter how many times I have read it, and I have probably read it well over 100 times, it still blows my mind how simple the message is... and how clear it is that he was talking about BELIEF and how our reality takes form.

The law of BELIEF is the only law of expression.

*"BELIEF IS the way".*

*"BELIEF IS the resurrection".*

BELIEF is the way as well as the power which resurrects and expresses all that man will ever be conscious of being.

Turn from the blindness of the uninitiated man who attempts to express and possess those qualities and things which he DOES NOT BELIEVE HE IS OR HAS; and be as the illumined mystic who BELIEVES on the basis of this changeless law.

Consciously BELIEVE yourself to be that which you seek; appropriate the consciousness of that which you see; and you too will know the status of the true mystic, as follows:

I became A BELIEVER of being it. I am still BELIEVER of being it. And I shall continue to be a BELIEVER of being it until that which I BELIEVE I am is perfectly expressed.

*"Yes, I BELIEVE a thing and it COMES to pass."*

When I first read that with "new eyes" It felt like I had pierced that thin veil that has kept the truth from me. I finally had an understanding that would allow me to permanently change my life for the better.

I SIMPLY had to pay attention to what I was always thinking, always saying and what I was agreeing with as being true for me.. KNOWING that my BELIEFS are and have been creating my reality.

*"Ye shall know the truth,
and the truth shall make you free."*

**The truth that sets man free is the knowledge that his consciousness is the resurrection and the life, that his consciousness both resurrects and makes alive all that he is conscious of being." - Neville**

*"Ye shall know the truth,
and the truth shall make you free."*

The truth that sets man free is the knowledge that his BELIEFS ARE the resurrection and the life, that his BELIEFS both resurrects and makes alive all that he BELIEVES HIMSELF TO BE.

Over the years I became VERY conscious of the importance of understanding the definitions of certain words as they apply to these teachings. I knew it was the difference between understanding what I was reading and only thinking I understood. I knew I understood WHEN I was able to apply what I interpreted and get actual results.

No one can prove these teachings to another. They can only be proven to self. All anyone can do is point the way. It is up to the individual whether or not they are willing to accept the instructions and test them for themselves.

As I was making this discovery, as it became a revelation to me that our beliefs create our reality, I was excited, I was amazed and my mind was blown. It was as if all the reading and studying I had invested in had finally paid off its biggest dividends. I was reaping the rewards and benefits that I felt had been promised to those who "applied this secret".

**"When it is recorded that Jesus left the world and went to His Father it is simply stating that He turned His attention from the world of the senses and rose in consciousness to that level which He desired to express.**

**There He remained until He became one with the consciousness to which He ascended. When He returned to the world of man, He could act with the positive assurance of that which He was conscious of being, a state of consciousness no one but Himself felt or knew that He possessed.**

**Man who is ignorant of this everlasting law of expression looks upon such happenings as miracles.**

**To rise in consciousness to the level of the thing desired and to remain there until such level becomes your nature is the way of all seeming miracles." - Neville**

This may sound good.. and I know it does. But let's be clear, he isn't talking about Jesus. He is talking about applying a law, a creative principle that ALL of us can apply and get results from.

When it is recorded that Jesus left the world and went to His Father it is simply stating that He turned His attention from the world of the senses and FOCUSD ON HIS CHOSEN BELIEFS which He desired to express.

There He remained until He became one with the THOUGHTS to which He BELIEVED. When He returned to the world of SENSE, He could act with the positive assurance of that which He FELT TO BE TRUE, a BELIEF THAT no one but Himself felt or knew that He possessed.

Man who is ignorant of this everlasting law of expression (The Law of BELIEF) looks upon such happenings as miracles.

To rise TO THE LEVEL OF BELIEVING YOUR DESIRE IS ALREADY FULFILLED and to remain there until such level becomes your nature is the way of all seeming miracles.

### *"I and My Father are one."*

**My consciousness is the Father who draws the manifestation of life to me.**

**The nature of the manifestation is determined by the state of consciousness in which I dwell. I am always drawing into my world that which I am conscious of being.**

**If you are dissatisfied with your present expression of life, then you must be born again.**

**Rebirth is the dropping of that level with which you are dissatisfied and rising to that level of consciousness which you desire to express and possess.**

You cannot serve two masters or opposing states of consciousness at the same time. Taking your attention from one state and placing it upon the other, you die to the one from which you have taken it and you live and express the one with which you are united.

Man cannot see how it would be possible to express that which he desires to be by so simple a law as acquiring the consciousness of the thing desired.

The reason for this lack of faith on the part of man is that he looks at the desired state through the consciousness of his present limitations. Therefore, he naturally sees it as impossible of accomplishment.

One of the first things man must realize is that it is impossible, in dealing with this spiritual law of consciousness,

*"to put new wine into old bottles or new patches on old garments."*

That is, you cannot take any part of the present consciousness into the new state. For the state sought is complete in itself and needs no patching. Every level of consciousness automatically expresses itself.

To rise to the level of any state is to automatically become that state in expression. But, in order to rise to the level that you are not now expressing, you must completely drop the consciousness with which you are now identified.

Until your present consciousness is dropped, you will not be able to rise to another level." - Neville

This is ALL about your BELIEFS creating your reality.

*"I and My Father are one."*

My BELIEFS ARE the Father who draws the manifestation of life to me.

The nature of the manifestation is determined by the BELIEFS WHICH I CONTINUALLY THINK ABOUT. I am always drawing into my world that which I BELIEVE I AM.

If you are dissatisfied with your present expression of life, then you must be born again.

Rebirth is the dropping of BELIEFS which you are dissatisfied and BELIEVING THAT which you desire to express and possess.

You cannot serve two masters or BELIEFS at the same time. Taking your attention from one BELIEF and placing it upon the other BELIEF, you die to the one from which you have taken it and you live and express the one with which you are united.

Man cannot see how it would be possible to express that which he desires to be by so simple a law as acquiring the THOUGHT THAT HIS BELIEF IS FULFILLED.

The reason for this lack of faith on the part of man is that he looks at the desired state through the BELIEF of his present limitations. Therefore, he naturally sees it as impossible of accomplishment.

One of the first things man must realize is that it is impossible, in dealing with this spiritual law of consciousness, *"to put new wine into old bottles or new patches on old garments."*

That is, you cannot take any part of YOUR LIMITING BELIEFS into YOUR NEW BELIEFS. For the state sought is complete in itself and needs no patching. Every level of BELIEF automatically expresses itself.

To BELIEVE ANYTHING TO BE TRUE FOR YOU is to automatically become that state in expression. But, in order to rise to THAT BELIEF that you are not now expressing, you must completely drop the BELIEF with which you are now identified.

Until your present LIMITING BELIEF is dropped, you will not be able to rise to THE DESIRED BELIEF.

**"If ye believe not that I AM He, ye shall die in your sins."**

**Unless man discovers that his consciousness is the cause of every expression of his life, he will continue seeking the cause of his confusion in the world of effects, and so shall die in his fruitless search." - Neville**

*"If ye believe not that I AM He, ye shall die in your sins."*

Unless man discovers that his BELIEFS ARE the cause of every expression of his life, he will continue seeking the cause of his confusion in the world of effects, and so shall die in his fruitless search.

Neville used the word Consciousness many times throughout his writings. But without being able to define what he meant by this, that really doesn't tell us as much as you think it does. I repeat this again... Consciousness is modified by our beliefs. Knowing this, we have defined consciousness. Now we KNOW how to interpret his writings.

**"Consciousness being Lord and Master, you are the Master Magician conjuring that which you are now conscious of being." - Neville**

YOUR BELIEFS being Lord and Master, you are the Master Magician conjuring that which you are now conscious of BELIEVING TO BE TRUE FOR YOU.

**"Consciousness precedes all manifestations and is the prop upon which all manifestation rests. To remove the manifestations, all that is required of you, the conceiver, is to take your attention away from the conception.**

**Instead of "Out of sight, out of mind", it really is "Out of mind, out of sight"." - Neville**

YOUR BELIEFS precede all manifestations and is the prop upon which all manifestation rests. To remove the manifestations, all that is required of you, the conceiver, is to take your attention away from BELIEVING WHAT YOU BELIEVED THAT CREATED WHAT YOU NO LONGER DESIRE.

Instead of "Out of sight, out of mind", it really is "Out of mind, out of sight".

*"I can of Myself do nothing,*
*the Father within Me,*
*He doeth the work"*

**"When man wills, he attempts to make something which does not now exist appear in time and space. Too often we are not aware of that which we are**

really doing. We unconsciously state that we do not possess the capacities to express. We predicate our desire upon the hope of acquiring the necessary capacities in future time.

"I AM not, but I will be".

Man does not realize that consciousness is the Father which does the work, so he attempts to express that which he is not conscious of being.

Such struggles are doomed to failure; only the present expresses itself. Unless I am conscious of being that which I seek, I will not find it.

God (your awareness) is the substance and fullness of all." - Neville

*"I can of Myself do nothing,
the Father within Me,
He doeth the work"*

When man wills, he attempts to make something which does not now exist appear in time and space. Too often we are not aware of that which we are really doing. We unconsciously BELIEVE that we do not possess the capacities to express. We predicate our desire upon the hope of acquiring the necessary capacities in future time.

"I AM not, but I will be".

Man does not realize that ALL THAT HE BELIEVES is the Father which does the work, so he attempts to express that which he is not conscious of being.

Such struggles are doomed to failure; only the present expresses itself. Unless I am conscious of BELIEVING I AM that which I seek, I will not find it.

God (your BELIEF) is the substance and fullness of all.

*"To him that hath it shall be given and to him that hath not it shall be taken away".*

"Though many look upon this statement as one of the most cruel and unjust of the sayings attributed to Jesus, it still remains a just and merciful law based upon life's changeless principle of expression.

Man's ignorance of the working of the law does not excuse him nor save him from the results.

Law is impersonal and therefore no respecter of persons. Man is warned to be selective in that which he hears and accepts as true. Everything that man accepts as true leaves an impression on his consciousness and must in time be defined as proof or disproof.

Perceptive hearing is the perfect medium through which man registers impressions. A man must discipline himself to hear only that which he wants to hear, regardless of rumors or the evidence of his senses to the contrary.

As he conditions his perceptive hearing, he will react only to those impressions which he has decided upon. This law never fails. Fully conditioned, man becomes incapable of hearing other than that which contributes to his desire." - Neville

*"To him that BELIEVES it shall be given*

*and to him that DOES not BELIEVE it shall be taken away".*

Though many look upon this statement as one of the most cruel and unjust of the sayings attributed to Jesus, it still remains a just and merciful law based upon life's changeless principle of expression.

Man's ignorance of the working of the LAW OF BELIEF does not excuse him nor save him from the results.

THE LAW OF BELIEF is impersonal and therefore no respecter of persons. Man is warned to be selective in that which he hears and BELIEVES TO BE true. Everything that man BELIEVES TO BE true leaves an impression IN HIS SUBCONSCIOUS MIND and must in time be defined as proof or disproof.

Perceptive hearing is the perfect medium through which man registers impressions. A man must discipline himself to BELIEVE only that which he wants to BELIEVE, regardless of rumors or the evidence of his senses to the contrary.

As he conditions his perceptive hearing, he will react only to those impressions which he has decided upon. THE LAW OF BELIEF never fails. Fully conditioned, man becomes incapable of BELIEVING other than that which contributes to his desire.

The more readily you are able to accept that this was what Neville was teaching throughout his books, the more you will be able to see it. It will amaze you how simple it really is, that no matter what words he used or what methods he spoke of, it all comes down to what you accept as being TRUE FOR YOU... what you BELIEVE. That is, and always has created your individual world.

Remember, It's HOW we think that matters.

> "Once man accepts **THINKING FROM THE END** as a **CREATIVE PRINCIPLE** in which he can cooperate, then he is redeemed from the absurdity of ever attempting to achieve his objective by merely thinking of it." - Neville Goddard

With a working knowledge of The Law of Belief and working in harmony with it you can fulfill all your dreams.

## Metaphysical / Law of Attraction Books

Neville Goddard's Interpretation of Scripture (2018)

The Neville Goddard Collection (All 10 of his books plus 2 Lecture series) (2016)

The Secret of Imagination, Imagination Fulfills itself: 12 Lectures On The Creative Power of Imagination (2021)

The Story Of Jesus Is Persistent Assumption: A Metaphysical Interpretation of Scripture (2021)

Neville Goddard - Assumptions Harden Into Facts: The Book (2016)

Neville Goddard - Imagination: The Redemptive Power in Man (2016)

Neville Goddard - The World is At Your Command - The Very Best of Neville Goddard (2017)

Neville Goddard - Imagining Creates Reality - 365 Mystical Daily Quotes (2017)

David Allen - The Power of I AM (2014), The Power of I AM - Volume 2 (2015), The Power of I AM - Volume 3 (2017)

David Allen - The Creative Power of Thought, Man's Greatest Discovery (2017)

David Allen - The Secrets, Mysteries & Powers of The Subconscious Mind (2017)

David Allen - The Money Bible - The Secrets of Attracting Prosperity (2017)

David Allen - Your Faith Is Your Fortune, Your Unlimited Power (2018)

The Definitive Christian D. Larson Collection (6 Volumes, 30 books) (2014)

Visit us at **NevilleGoddardBooks.com** for 1000's of Free Downloadable eBooks on Metaphysics, Law of Attraction, Oriental Philosophy, Ancient Secrets, plus much more.

## Suggested Reading

Claude Bristol - The Magic of Believing

Neville Goddard - Prayer: The Art Of Believing

Robert Collier - "The Secret of the Ages"

Robert Collier - "The Secret of Gold"

Napoleon Hill - "Think and Grow Rich"

Annie Rix Militz - Prosperity Through the Knowledge and Power of Mind

Joseph Murphy - Your Infinite Power to Be Rich

Anthony Norvell - Money Magnetism - How to Grow Rich Beyond Your Wildest Dreams

Franklyn Hobbs - The Secret of Wealth

Benjamin Franklin - The Way to Wealth

Julia Seton Sears M.D. - The Key to Health, Wealth and Love

Charles Fillmore - Prosperity

John Seaman Garns - Prosperity Plus

Franklin Fillmore Farrington - Realizing Prosperity

Florence Barnard - The Prosperity Book

James Allen - Eight Pillars of Prosperity

Bernard C. Ruggles - Creative Abundance; The Psychology of Ability and Plenty

## Notes

www.ingramcontent.com/pod-product-compliance
Lightning Source LLC
Chambersburg PA
CBHW030917080526
44589CB00010B/342